BOOK OF BEGINNING TROMBONE SOLOS

Edited by **Eugene Watts** of The Canadian Brass

■

All Selections Performed by **Eugene Watts** on trombone, and pianist Bill Casey

■

Plus Piano Accompaniments Only

Arranged by Bill Boyd

CONTENTS

The instrument pictured on the cover is a CB20 Trombone from The Canadian Brass Collection, a line of professional brass instruments marketed by The Canadian Brass.

Photo: Gordon Janowiak

To access audio, visit:
www.halleonard.com/mylibrary

Enter Code
1003-5416-0403-4549

HAL•LEONARD®

7777 W. BLUEMOUND RD. P.O. BOX 13819 MILWAUKEE, WI 53213

www.canadianbrass.com
www.halleonard.com

Dear Fellow Brass Player:

We might be just a little biased, but we believe that playing a brass instrument is one of the most positive activities that anyone can pursue. Whether you're 8 years old or 60 years old, the ability to play a horn automatically creates opportunities of playing with other people in bands, orchestras, and ensembles throughout your life. But to keep yourself in shape and to better your playing, it's important to regularly work at solos. You might perform a contest solo for school, or play for a church service, or just for your family in the living room. Here's a book full of solos, in varied styles, that we think you'll enjoy learning.

All this music has been recorded for you by The Canadian Brass and is available to you online using the unique code found on page 1. Each song is provided twice: once as a full performance that includes the piano accompaniment and the solo instrument, and the other as the piano accompaniment only, which you can use in your practice, or if you wish, to perform with. The recordings of the solos that we have made should be used only as a guide in studying a piece. We certainly didn't go into these recording sessions with the idea of trying to create any kind of "definitive performances" of this music. There is no such thing as a definitive performance anyway. Each musician, being a unique individual, will naturally always come up with a slightly different rendition of a piece of music. We often find that students are timid about revealing their own ideas and personalities when going beyond the notes on the page in making music. After you've practiced for weeks on a piece of music, and have mastered all the technical requirements, you certainly have earned the right to play it in the way you think it sounds best! It may not be the way your friend would play it, or the way The Canadian Brass would play it. But you will have made the music your own, and that's what counts.

Good luck and Happy Brass Playing!
The Canadian Brass

EUGENE WATTS was born and raised in Sedalia, Missouri (the home of Scott Joplin). Like the story of *The Music Man*, a traveling instrument salesman convinced his parents that Gene would make a great euphonium player. He soon switched to trombone and started playing in taverns and nightclubs, steeping himself in a jazz and Dixieland tradition. He worked his way through college at the University of Missouri with his own Dixieland band, "The Missouri Mudcats." Further studies followed with Arnold Jacobs. He established an orchestral career in a succession of positions with the North Carolina, the San Antonio, and the Milwaukee Symphonies, and was asked by Seiji Ozawa to become principal trombone of the Toronto Symphony. While in Toronto, his intense interest in chamber music led to the founding of The Canadian Brass. Beyond his musical career, Gene is a continuing student of transcendental meditation.

BILL CASEY, pianist, grew up in Atlanta, and holds degrees in piano from Louisiana State University and the University of Missouri at Kansas City. He was assistant editor on the new G. Schirmer Opera Anthology, and has recorded several other albums for Hal Leonard. He resides in Kansas City, where he runs a music school for piano and voice students, as well as continuing to perform as both a pianist and singer.

CANADIAN BRASS BLUES

Bill Boyd

YANKEE DOODLE

Traditional American

STREETS OF LAREDO

American Folksong (adapted from old Irish air)

ODE TO JOY

Adapted from Symphony No. 9
by Ludwig van Beethoven

AMERICA

Words by Samuel F. Smith
Music by Henry Carey

CARNIVAL OF VENICE

Julius Benedict

THE RIDDLE SONG

English ballad

FINLANDIA

Jean Sibelius

CANADIAN BRASS BLUES

TROMBONE

Bill Boyd

Moderately

YANKEE DOODLE

Traditional American

Moderately

2

STREETS OF LAREDO

American Folksong (adapted from old Irish air)

Moderately

mf smoothly

rit.

ODE TO JOY

Adapted from Symphony No. 9
by Ludwig van Beethoven

Moderately

mp smoothly

mf

f

rit.

AMERICA

Words by Samuel F. Smith
Music by Henry Carey

CARNIVAL OF VENICE

Julius Benedict

THE RIDDLE SONG

English ballad

Moderately

FINLANDIA

Jean Sibelius

Moderately

AMAZING GRACE

Words by John Newton
Traditional American melody

THE SKATERS

Emil Wauldteufel

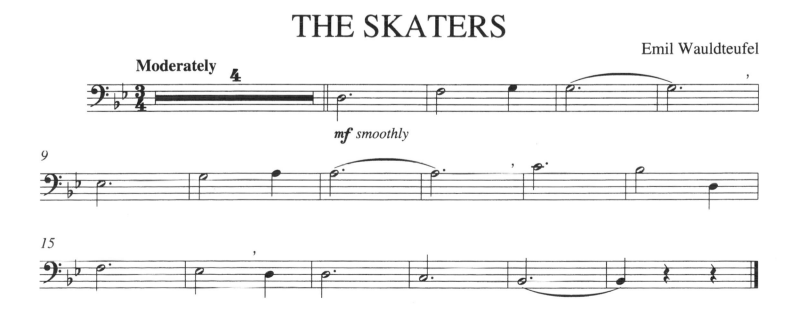

6

MARINE'S HYMN

Words by unknown marine (1847)
Music by Jacques Offenbach

TAKE ME OUT TO THE BALL GAME

Words by Jack Norworth
Music by Albert von Tilzer

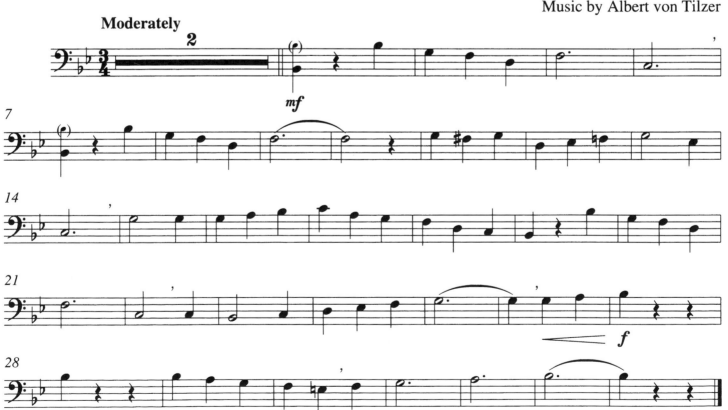

SONG OF THE VOLGA BOATMAN

Russian Folksong

THE CRUEL WAR IS RAGING

American Folksong

DOXOLOGY

Words by Thomas Ken
Music by Louis Bourgéois

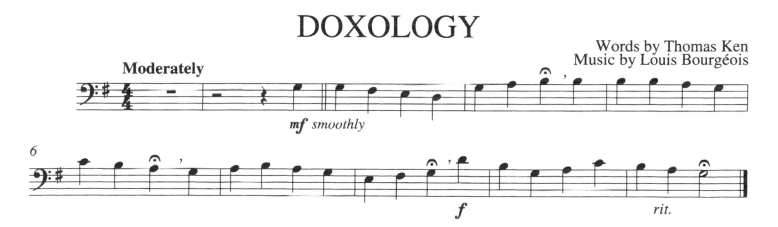

GIVE MY REGARDS TO BROADWAY

Words and Music by George M. Cohan

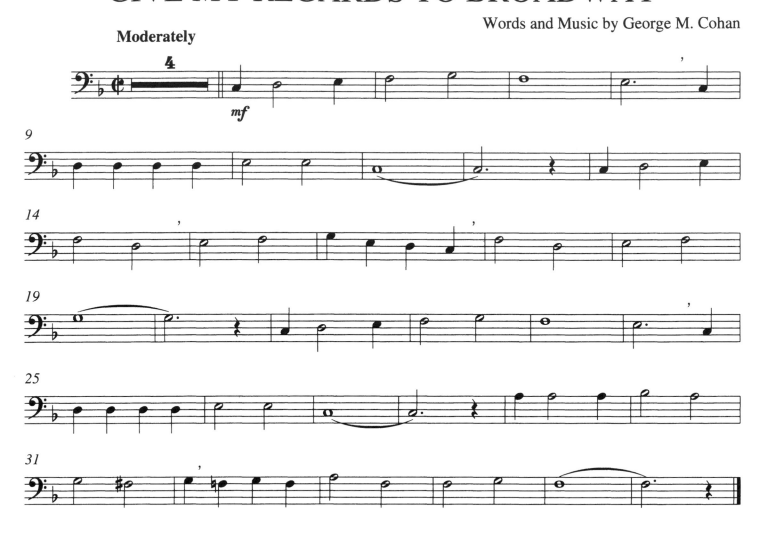

JUST A CLOSER WALK

Words and Music by Red Foley

AMAZING GRACE

Words by John Newton
Traditional American melody

THE SKATERS

Emil Wauldteufel

MARINE'S HYMN

Words by unknown marine (1847)
Music by Jacques Offenbach

TAKE ME OUT TO THE BALL GAME

Words by Jack Norworth
Music by Albert von Tilzer

SONG OF THE VOLGA BOATMAN

Russian Folksong

THE CRUEL WAR IS RAGING

American Folksong

DOXOLOGY

Words by Thomas Ken
Music by Louis Bourgéois

GIVE MY REGARDS TO BROADWAY

Words and Music by George M. Cohan

JUST A CLOSER WALK

Words and Music by Red Foley